CONTENTS

KU-220-443

Becoming a master

Imagine being able to break bricks with your bare hands, leap in the air and kick two people at once, or throw someone to the ground with a flick of the wrist! That's what it's like being a martial arts master.

Martial arts are fun for all. These kids are studying karate in Vietnam.

Don't try this at home!

If you want to learn how to do martial arts, find a qualified coach. Never just try to do something you've seen in a movie or a book. You could hurt yourself or someone else.

For thousands of years, martial arts experts revealed their secrets only to a few lucky students. Today, almost anyone can learn martial arts. Even so, becoming a master takes years of experience.

muscles body parts that allow your bones to move

POWER OF KICK

POWER OF KICK

Look out for this jumping double-kick in the movie Crouching Tiger, Hidden Dragon.

For martial arts, your **muscles**, heart, lungs, and **reflexes** must all be trained to perfection. Only then will you be ready to deliver the powerful punches, kicks and throws of a master.

reflex an automatic muscle reaction

The secret of youth

Would you believe that martial arts help to keep you young? If you don't believe it, look at Lucille Thompson. She was the oldest person to get a black belt in taekwondo – at 88!

Many martial arts masters live a long time. Their tough training has lots of benefits:

• Using your muscles every day keeps them strong.
• Practice fights work your heart and lungs hard, making them fitter.
• Stretching your muscles while practising keeps them **flexible**.

This Kung Fu master is really flexible for his age.

Older martial artists might not be as fast or as strong as their young students, but they are very skilled. Years of practice mean they can often easily beat a younger fighter.

black belt an expert level in martial arts   **flexible** able to bend easily

Martial arts actor Jet Li, mid-way through an axe kick in one of his movies.

Force of kick

Uh-oh!

Body is upright for good balance.

force a push or a pull

Power punches

CRUNCH!

Some martial artists can throw a punch so fast you can barely see it – at least, not without a slow-motion camera to help! How do they manage it?

To punch hard, you have to be well balanced. Martial artists call this having a good **stance**. Punching power comes from your whole body, not just your fist – all the way from your feet, through your body, along your arm and… BOOM!

There are two basic types of punch. Straight punches travel the shortest possible distance to the target, and are fast. Hook punches travel in a curved path and are very powerful.

Karate fighters use mostly straight, fast punches.

stance position of the body

Stance matters

Some martial arts teachers say: "No stance, no chance!" because stance is so important.

Muhammad Ali (right) was one of the be boxers who ever lived.

4 Right on **the button!**

2 Muscles in shoulders and arms give strength.

Hook punch comes up from below.

1 Muscles in back leg power the punch.

the button boxers sometimes call the chin "the button"

Getting your kicks

Do you know which is the strongest muscle in your body? It's in your leg, at the front of your **thigh**. Martial artists use this muscle (the *quadriceps femoris*) in their most powerful moves – kicks.

*A karate expert lands a high **roundhouse** kick.*

It takes a lot of training to learn to kick well. To become an expert you need:
- Good balance, or you just fall over and look silly.
- To be able to aim the kick properly.
- Flexible hip, leg and foot muscles, so that the kick can travel all the way to your target.

thigh the upper part of your leg, above the knee   **roundhouse** a kick that travels in a curve

If you need both legs to kick with, what do you stand on?

Cat fight

There is an old **British** sport called "purring". It's not very hard to learn – you kick each other in the shins until one of you gives in!

Pushing on a stick helps to keep the fighter in the air.

Thigh muscles **contract**, pulling the foot up and around.

Flexible muscles at the back of the legs allow the kick to reach the target.

contract to shrink or tighten

Flying high

Some martial artists have a kick as hard as a horse's! In fact, they can kick so high and hard, they can knock a man OFF a horse. How on Earth do they manage that?

Really powerful kicks use jumps and spins. They work because the attacker uses the jump or spin to add extra force to the kick. The opponent gets hit not only by powerful leg muscles, but also by the energy contained in the movement.

Some of the most powerful kicks of all use both a jump AND a spin. Power of kick + power of jump + power of spin = OUCH! If you see a jumping, spinning kick coming, duck!

A jumping, spinning, roundhouse kick!

Off the wall

Hapkido students learn to jump up and bounce off a wall to launch a high kick.

High jumping kicks are sometimes called **flying kicks**. You can see why!

POW!

FORCE OF KICK

Force of kick is concentrated in the heel.

Leg muscles add power.

flying kick a high jumping kick that travels a long way

Close-up crunches

Bruce Lee knees his co-star Chuck Norris in the movie The Way of the Dragon.

You might think that grabbing hold of a martial artist would mean he or she can't hit you. You'd be wrong! Even up close, martial artists can land a powerful blow.

Martial artists strike with their knees and elbows if they're too close to make a good kick or punch. Thai boxers are trained to grab opponents by the neck and pull them onto a knee strike. Or they jump up and knee the opponent in the head — that's called a "flying knee"!

Strikes like these work well when they bring hard bone into contact with softer parts of the body. Getting an elbow in the stomach, for example, is bad news!

Not-so-funny bone!

The elbow is one of the hardest bones in your body. It's hard to hurt yourself by elbowing someone.

pivot to turn around a fixed point

Ow!

Kickboxer Daniel Dawson lands a powerful knee strike during a World Championship match.

4 Opponent falls back.

3 Knee strike

2 Knee comes up.

1 Dawson pivots on one leg.

No choke

Imagine being able to weaken your opponent in seconds, forcing him or her to give up and let you win! Amazingly, many martial artists can do this – but how?

A fighter tries to get a chokehold on his opponent.

Your brain and muscles need oxygen to keep working. One of the fastest ways to win in martial arts is to (temporarily) cut off your opponent's oxygen supply. The secret is a **choke** or **strangle**.

choke stopping someone from breathing **strangle** cutting off blood from the brain

1 Arms lock tightly around the neck to apply the choke.

3 Blood supply to the brain is cut off.

2 It is hard to breathe oxygen into the lungs.

4 Fighter defends by pushing her chin down hard.

Once a wrestler gets a good choke on you there's not much you can do about it!

Chokes and strangles MUST be done properly. Knowing when to stop is vital, so martial artists learn a signal called **tapping out**. Even if two fighters don't speak the same language, they know that a tap of the fingers means to let go right away!

WARNING! CHOKES AND STRANGLES ARE VERY DANGEROUS. Never use them unless you are being supervised by a martial arts master.

tapping out tapping your opponent or the ground to show you give up

All locked up

Taking control of a stronger opponent can be very hard work. But martial arts masters can do it with almost no effort – using special techniques called joint locks.

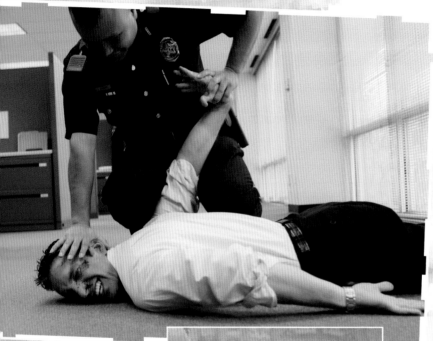

Police officers often use joint locks to control their suspects.

Our joints are designed to bend in particular directions. The elbow, for example, only goes backwards and forwards. When a joint is forced in the wrong direction, it really hurts!

Martial arts masters have worked out ways of "locking" their opponents' joints. This means forcing them into a painful position. Joint locks are normally done on the arm or wrist. Once you're trapped in a good joint lock, it's VERY difficult to escape.

Ouch!

Joint locks hurt because they take the joint outside its normal range of motion.

joint a part of the body where two bones are connected

*The judo player on his back is performing a flying **arm bar**.*

1 Hold the arm firmly between the legs.

3 Straighten your legs to make it hurt even more!

2 Pull on the arm like a lever.

Aaaagh!

arm bar a kind of arm lock where the arm is straight

Go throw

Boxers have a saying: "A good big 'un always beats a good little 'un." They mean that if everything else is equal, the biggest fighter wins. But not if they're up against a martial arts throwing master!

Throwing an opponent, especially a bigger one, is easiest if you throw them the way they're already going. Using their own movement means that your muscles need only to guide their fall – **gravity** helps with the rest.

Your sense of balance helps you to stay upright. If you can tip someone over or pull their feet out from under them, they lose their balance and start to fall. Gravity will soon make sure they end up on the floor!

Wrestlers will try anything to throw one another to the ground!

Demolition zone

In judo, breaking an opponent's balance is called *kuzushi*. The name is based on the Japanese word meaning: "to pull down, or demolish".

gravity a force that attracts objects to each other, especially towards Earth

Wrestler grips his opponent and turns this way.

Opponent loses his balance and starts to fall.

GRAVITY

21

Master-fall

You might think that after being thrown by a martial arts master, the fight would be over. But if you've learned your lessons properly, you can be back on your feet in the blink of an eye.

*The **judoka** in blue is using ukemi skills to avoid being hurt by this throw.*

DIRECTION OF THROW

1 The fighter tucks in her head.

2 She brings her shoulder forwards and in.

Falls, or *ukemi*, are almost the first thing a new judo fighter learns. *Ukemi* are designed to make sure the fighter's spine, neck and head cannot be injured in a fall.

Ukemi work by spreading out the energy of a throw. Not only the body, but also the arms, legs, hands and feet are used to **absorb** the force of the throw.

Belly-gazing

One way to make sure your head is properly tucked in is to look at your belt knot.

Banging your arm and hand down on the mat gets rid of some of the energy of the throw.

Wham!

judoka the name for a judo fighter   **absorb** to soak up or take in

Eating your way to the top

Eating the right food is important for everyone, but some people need more food than others to do their jobs. Sumo wrestlers are the giants of the martial arts world – for a reason!

A boxer takes a drink between rounds. Drinking plenty of water is crucial: without it, the body stops performing properly.

We all need **nutritious** food to grow, be healthy and have energy. But the amount of food a giant sumo eats is amazing. Normal-sized men need about 2,500 **calories** a day. Sumos eat over three times as much!

Sumos use their extra weight to give them power in the ring. They leap forwards, trying to force each other to fall. What looks suspiciously like two fat men leaning on each other is actually a very skilled martial art.

nutritious rich in vitamins, minerals and other ingredients that keep us healthy

EXTRA CALORIES =
EXTRA WEIGHT

Smaller sumo aims to
unbalance the larger one,
so his weight acts against
him and makes him fall.

Huge muscles propel the sumo forwards.

Extra weight
adds power to
the movement.

Mega-weight

One of the heaviest sumo wrestlers
ever was the Hawaiian sumo
Konishki. He weighed 238 kilograms
(37.5 stone) and was nicknamed
"The Dump Truck".

*Two sumo wrestlers launch
at each other at a signal
from the referee.*

calories a measure of the energy in food

Smashing stuff

Many martial artists are experts at punching and kicking. But how do they test just how expert they are? One way is by seeing how many boards, bricks and other objects they can smash – with their **BARE HANDS!**

Breaking boards, bricks or paving slabs is a skill that needs a lot of practice. Wood is stronger than a person's hand or foot, so it's important to get it right. Concrete and brick are even harder!

It takes special training to smash stuff with your body and not get hurt. The trick is to hit the target dead-centre and to push through. If you hit too close to the edge, the object won't break – but your hand might!

A taekwondo black belt breaks boards with a flying kick.

Wreckage race

In Demolition and Destruction competitions, teams of martial artists race to see who can destroy a house fastest, using just their hands and feet!

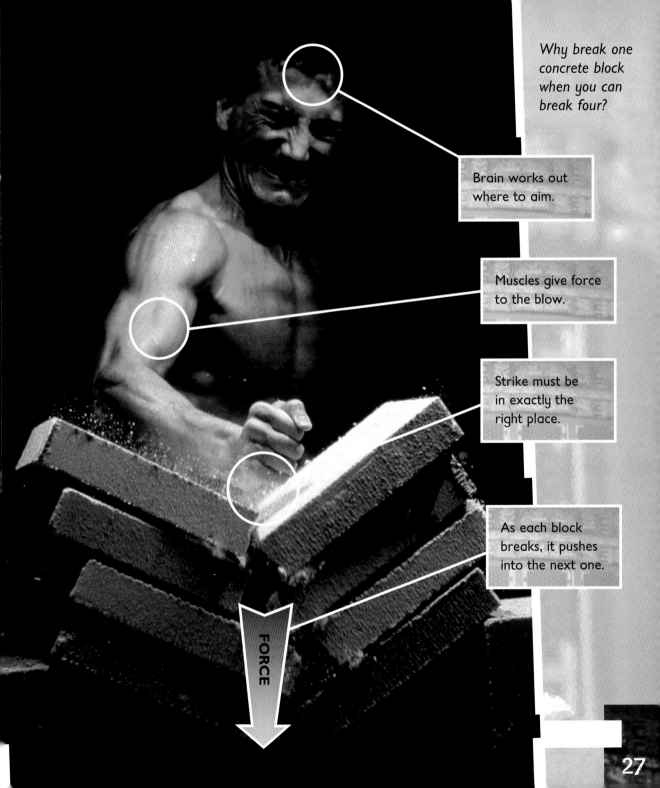

Why break one concrete block when you can break four?

Brain works out where to aim.

Muscles give force to the blow.

Strike must be in exactly the right place.

As each block breaks, it pushes into the next one.

FORCE

27

Olympic masters

When the Olympics come to London in 2012, medals in boxing, judo, taekwondo and wrestling will all be up for grabs. Some previous gold medallists became legends who inspired others.

Name: Muhammad Ali
Born: 1942
Nationality: American
Ali won Olympic gold for boxing and won the world **heavyweight** title three times. He was named Sportsman of the Century in 1999.

Name: Kurt Angle
Born: 1968
Nationality: American
Angle won Olympic gold for wrestling in 1996. He went on to become world famous in wrestling shows like WWF and TNA Wrestling.

Name: Arlene Limas
Born: 1966
Nationality: American
Limas was the first American and the first woman to win Olympic gold in taekwondo.

Name: Ryoko Tani
Born: 1975
Nationality: Japanese
Tani is the greatest female judo player ever. She won gold at the Olympics twice and won the World Championships seven times in a row.

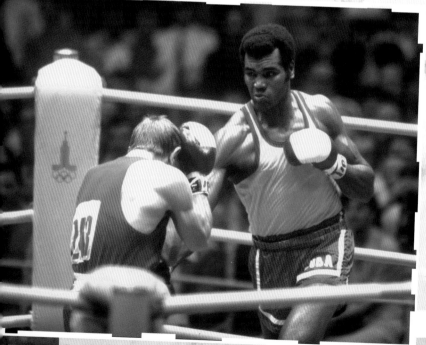

The great Cuban boxer Teofilo Stevenson in action at the 1980 Moscow Olympics. He was on his way to winning a record third gold medal in the heavyweight division.

1 Pull the opponent forward and off balance.

2 Hook his leg away and up high.

3 Gravity takes over.

4 He lands on his back in front of you!

Kosei Inoue (in white) won the gold medal at the 2000 Sydney Olympics with this throw.

heavyweight one of the highest weight divisions in martial arts

Glossary

absorb to soak up or take in

arm bar a kind of arm lock where the arm is straight

black belt an expert level in martial arts

button boxers sometimes call the chin "the button"

calories a measure of the energy in food

choke stopping someone from breathing

contract to shrink or tighten

flexible able to bend easily

flying kick a high jumping kick that travels a long way

force a push or a pull

gravity a force that attracts objects to each other, especially towards Earth

heavyweight one of the highest weight divisions in martial arts

joint a part of the body where two bones are connected

judoka the name for a judo fighter

muscles body parts that allow your bones to move

nutritious rich in vitamins, minerals and other ingredients that keep us healthy

pivot to turn around a fixed point

reflex an automatic muscle reaction

roundhouse a kick that travels in a curve

stance position of the body

strangle cutting off blood from the brain

tapping out tapping your opponent or the ground to show you give up

thigh the upper part of your leg, above the knee

Further information

Books

***Jun Fan/Jeet Kune Do –
Scientific Streetfighting*** by
Lamar M Davis II (HNL
Publishing, 1999)
A great guide with plenty
of photos, showing how to
use Bruce Lee's martial
art "Jeet Kune Do" for
self defence.

Martial Arts for Dummies
by Jennifer Lawler (For
Dummies, 2002)
An introduction to various
aspects of the martial arts
and what you can expect if
you decide to learn one.

The A–Z of Judo by Syd
Hoare (Ippon Books, 1994)
An excellent guide to
the throwing and
groundfighting techniques
of judo.

The Art of Striking by
Marc Tedeschi (Weatherhill
Inc, 2002)
Loads of photos and text
explaining many, many
different ways of hitting
and kicking people.

See also ***The Art of
Throwing*** and ***The Art of
Ground Fighting*** in the
same series.

Websites

**www.britishjudocouncil.
org**
The British Judo Council
organizes competitions
and runs clubs throughout
the UK.

www.tkd-itf.org
The International
Taekwondo Federation
promotes the sport of
taekwondo worldwide.

**www.
selfdefencefederation.
co.uk**
The Self Defence
Federation is an all-styles
self defence and martial
arts organization. It runs
courses for adults and
children all over the UK.

www.wakoweb.com
The World Association of
Kickboxing Organizations.
Photos and information on
a variety of disciplines from
full-contact fighting to
musical kata competitions.

Films

***Crouching Tiger, Hidden
Dragon*** directed by Ang
Lee (Warner Brothers/Sony
Pictures, 2000)
A spectacular martial arts
movie, famous for its use
of "wire work" – invisible
wires that allow the actors
to run up walls and through
the air. Features lots of
martial arts fights.

Hero directed by Yimou
Zhang (20th Century Fox,
2002)
Another spectacular
martial arts movie, this
time featuring a plot to
assassinate the king of Qin.
The nameless hero has
developed a technique that
can kill anyone if he gets
within ten paces of them!

Index